Elisabeth Pfeiffer

Pop & Rock-Ukulele

Strumming

Volume I

Published by Elisabeth Pfeiffer

ISBN: 9781505774825

Copyright © 2015 Elisabeth

All rights reserved. No part of this publication may be reproduced, stored in a retrieval system, or transmitted in any form or by any means, without the prior permission in writing from the publisher. The publisher is not responsible for websites (or their content) that are not owned by the publisher.

Title: Pop & Rock Ukulele: Strumming
Revised 3rd Edition January 2019
Author: Elisabeth Pfeiffer

Layout, Score and Photo-Illustrations: Elisabeth Pfeiffer
Picture 17, "Right Hand" by Freepik licensed by CC BY 3.0, edited by Elisabeth Pfeiffer
Publisher:
Elisabeth Pfeiffer
Ablestr. 23
84508 Burgkirchen
Germany

Videos, Audio Recordings and Mastering: Elisabeth Pfeiffer
Ukulele: by Susing's Guitars, Abuno, Pajac Lapulapu City 6015, Cebu Philippines

Elisabeth Pfeiffer

Pop & Rock-Ukulele

Strumming

Volume I

About the author

Elisabeth Pfeiffer majored in classical guitar, both at Lawrence University, Appleton, WI, USA and Hochschule für Musik, Würzburg, Germany, where she graduated in 2007. On a trip around the world, which lasted over 10 months, she got to know and love the Ukulele. Elisabeth spent more than ten years teaching guitar playing and thanks to that experience she is now able to spend her time exploring innovative aspects of the ukulele. She plays arrangements from Renaissance music to Jazz and is working on expanding the solo repertoire for the ukulele with her own arrangements and compositions.

Other Books from Pop & Rock Ukulele

Pop & Rock Ukulele: Picking

Pop & Rock Ukulele Books in German

Pop- und Rock-Ukulele: Schlagmuster
Pop- und Rock-Ukulele: Zupfmuster
Pop- und Rock-Ukulele: Griffe und Akkorde

Pop- und Rock-Ukulele: Ukulele für Kids

Find more information on

www.poprockukulele.de

Table of Contents

Preface 9

Introduction 11

Chapter 1 - Basic Strumming 13

Accent and Tone — 13

Holding the Ukulele — 14

Strumming in 4/4 — 16

Modules for New Patterns in 4/4 — 30

Swing Patterns — 31

Strumming in 3/4 — 33

Modules for New Patterns in 3/4 — 35

Strumming in 6/8 — 38

Chapter 2 - Advanced Strumming 41

1/16th Note Strumming — 41

Flamenco Techniques — 46

Palm Mute - Muting with your strumming hand — 51

Strumming with "Special Effects" — 51

Enhanced Strumming - Flamenco-influenced Patterns — 52

Strumming with Percussion — 52

Strumming in Songs — 54

Chapter 3 – Technique Kit 57
Exercises for Your Fretting Hand   57
Tapping exercise   59
Chords   60
Chord Diagrams   60
Chords in 1st position   61
Barre chords   64
Practicing with a Metronome   66
Brain-optimized Practicing   68
Which Ukulele?   69

Appendix. 69
Different Ways of Tuning   70
Is my Ukulele Properly Fretted?   71
Comparing Unisons   71
Comparing Octaves   71
Useful Accessories   72
Slip-resistant Cloth   72
The Strap   73
The Guitar Strap   73
My Way of Holding the Ukulele   74
Tuner   74

Download 75

Get the Audio

The audio files for this book are available to download for free from **www.poprockukulele.de/downloads**.
Simply fill out the form, select this book title from the drop-down menu and click on the download link after sending the form.
We recommend that you download the files directly to your computer, not to your tablet and extract them there before adding them to your media library. You can then put them on your tablet, iPod or burn them to CD.
If you run into problems, write an email to **info@poprockukulele.de** and we'll get back to you!

Preface

The Ukulele has gained enormous popularity during the last few years. The Hawaiian Jake Shimabukuro exposed the Ukulele with his Arrangement of George Harrisons „While my guitar gently weeps", which went viral on YouTube. Ever since then he has become very successful and has inspired others to dedicate time to the instrument.
George Harrison himself said the following about the Ukulele decades ago:

"Everyone should have a UKE. It's so simple to carry with you and its one instrument that you can't play and not laugh.

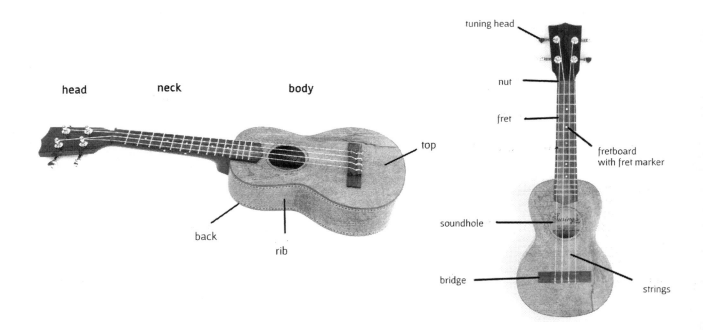

 Audio examples are numbered. Most of them contain the examples at different tempos - slow at first and then faster.

 You'll find the link to the video-playlist in the download.

 The „Uke it!" Icon indicates chord progressions that you can use to practice a certain strumming pattern. Those progressions are often harmonically open, so you can repeat them infinitely. The audio-tracks are also recorded, so you can play along.

 You can find the „technique kit" in the appendix. You'll find detailed information on techniques that are not immediately connected with picking. You'll find this symbol in the book, at spots when you can get more helpful information from the technique kit.

Introduction

It is fun to play the Ukulele, for both ourselves and our audience alike. We forget everything around us when we practice and find ourselves completely absorbed in the sound of the instrument.
The word ukulele means, „Jumping flee", and it is most known today for its defining role in Hawaiian music. Hearing it immediately conjures up images of palm trees and white, sandy beaches.

The ukulele originates from a version of the Portuguese guitar, called Braguinha. This Portuguese guitar is still prominently used in the Portuguese Fado. Back in the day, the steel string Braguinha, was brought to the new world by Portuguese sailors and modified so that it could be played with strings made from cat gut. Of course, today we play it with nylon strings, but there are still a few companies, such as Aquila, who try to imitate the sound of gut strings. These strings are widely used in "early music".
Over time, different tunings and various models of the ukulele have evolved. You can find more information about these variations in the appendix.
The Pop & Rock Ukulele series teaches you about many different aspects of Pop and Rock music and how these are performed on the ukulele. As well as basic and advanced techniques for picking and strumming, you'll find books on chords, chord structures, scales, solo repertoire, improvisation and much more.

Pop & Rock Ukulele: Strumming is about playing and constructing strumming patterns with basic chords and these techniques will be applied to your favourite songs.

You can download the audio tracks and view the videos for every volume online on

www.poprockukulele.de/downloads

Go to the download instruction on p. 75 to find the password you need to access the videos.

Don't hesitate to contact me for questions or concerns: *info@poprockukulele.de* .

Well, then, all that's left to say is; Have Fun!

Elisabeth

Chapter 1 - Basic Strumming

The ukulele is most commonly used as a rhythm instrument to accompany singers and other instrumentalists. Sometimes you'll sing by yourself or maybe you will be playing with another musician. To be a versatile musician you'll need to learn a wide variety of strumming patterns. Today, these patterns originate mostly from Rock and Pop guitar, but they have actually been used on stringed instruments for hundreds of years.

The Ukulele is a close relative of the lute (closer, in fact, than the guitar) and was strummed over 600 years ago. This book takes a detailed look at the most common strumming patterns that used today and these patterns are used in every Rock and Pop song you'll ever hear. Sometimes the original recorded strumming patterns are quite complicated, and we'll look at more advanced techniques in Chapter 2.

ACCENTS AND TONE

Before we get to the strumming patterns, we should briefly explore the concept of different meters or measures. Meter is the time structure of music, organized in bars with "strong" (accented) and "weak" (unaccented) beats. There are different ways to play these beats on the ukulele.

Strong beats are stroked downwards with the fingernail of the index finger (think "away from your body"). Weak beats are played with the nail of the thumb upwards (think "towards your head"). On weak beats it's not necessary to hit all strings. It is sufficient to play just two or three strings.

"away"

In the strumming patterns you'll see a ↓ indicating a "down" and a ↑ indicating an "up".

Always make contact with the strings using your nail, not your fingertip. If you use your fingertip to strum the strings, you'll create a very different sound.

"towards me"

At the end of Chapter 2 we'll look at strumming patterns that employ different tone colours, but you can of course experiment with different ways of strumming now and take note of the different colours you can produce.

HOLDING THE UKULELE

The "correct" way to hold your ukulele is often very personal, and also something, that will normally change over time.

A good playing position will allow both hands to have maximum freedom and a good range of movement. When playing the ukulele, one hand must always be on the instrument, which can lead to destabilization when performing complex strumming patterns.

Find a position where the weight of the ukulele can stay on your legs when you're sitting, allowing your strumming hand to move freely. The weight of the Ukulele should be held by a strap when you're standing. Your fretting hand should not contribute to stabilizing the instrument and under no circumstances "grab" or "carry" the ukulele.

If you're playing standing up without using accessories to support the ukulele, you should squeeze the ukulele with your right forearm (lefthanders: squeeze with your left forearm!), so that you can lift your fretting hand off the ukulele's neck.

A simple rule of thumb is that the way you hold the instrument should give you maximum freedom to move your hands. The small size of the ukulele and the weight of its head are obstacles on your journey towards a relaxed playing position.

As you advance, and as you begin to play pieces that are more difficult, there will be situations when you will have to decide whether the left or the right hand will hold the ukulele in a particular moment. Often the picking hand may have to help out when there are bigger shifts for the fretting hand. Here, the lightness of the ukulele is an advantage because it can easily be stabilized by just one finger. Coordination is everything!

Whether you decide to play in a standing or sitting position, there are different accessories that will make life easier. There are detailed descriptions of these in the appendix.

Chapter 1 - Basic Strumming

It is still uncommon to practice the ukulele for extended periods of time (more than 3hrs daily), but if you'd like to practice for that long on a regular basis, I can only applaud you and tell you that you're going to go a long way! If you're feeling inspired to experiment with different ideas for your position (i.e. a combination of strap and weights to keep the instrument in place), I encourage you to do so. Inspiration is welcome in the world of the ukulele and lots of players will be thankful.

Chapter 3 tells you about fretting hand basics and other important techniques and using the fretting hand is part of holding the ukulele properly.

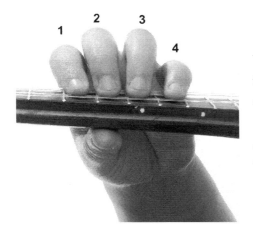

The fingers of the fretting hand are numbered and it's important to keep the thumb opposite the middle finger to balance and relax your hand on the fretboard.

A good fretting hand position will be helpful when you're working on the strumming patterns in this book.

Go to page 69 to learn more about the different ukulele types, how to tune your ukulele, and more.

STRUMMING IN 4/4

ACCENTS IN 4/4

Before examining the strumming patterns, we need to briefly explore 4/4 time. We've seen that the strong beats are played with down strokes and that weak beats are played with up strokes.

In addition to these strong and weak beats, each meter has natural accents that create different musical characters. The musical sign for an accent is '>'. I've used it in the following example to mark the natural accents in a bar containing four beats.

Every meter is accented on beat one. Beat one is usually the strongest accent in the bar. If there are two accents in a bar, the second one is normally weaker than the first. When you listen to the audio tracks always try playing along with them and try to match the different feels.

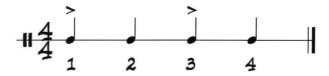

You can see an accent on "one" and "three" in the 4/4 bar above. A bar of 4/4 has two accents. You may have noticed that people (especially in Germany) often clap on the "one" and "three" in a bar of 4/4.

The one and three accents are "natural". These are not usually indicated, but rather taken for granted. In this book I will write accents only, when the accent is on a beat, which is not normally stressed. In most Rock and Pop music, however, the accent is on beats two and four.

The first example shows you how to strum on each beat of the bar. Each note in the bar lasts one beat or one quarter note and is played with a down strum. Listen to audio example 1 and try to play along rhythmically.

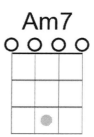

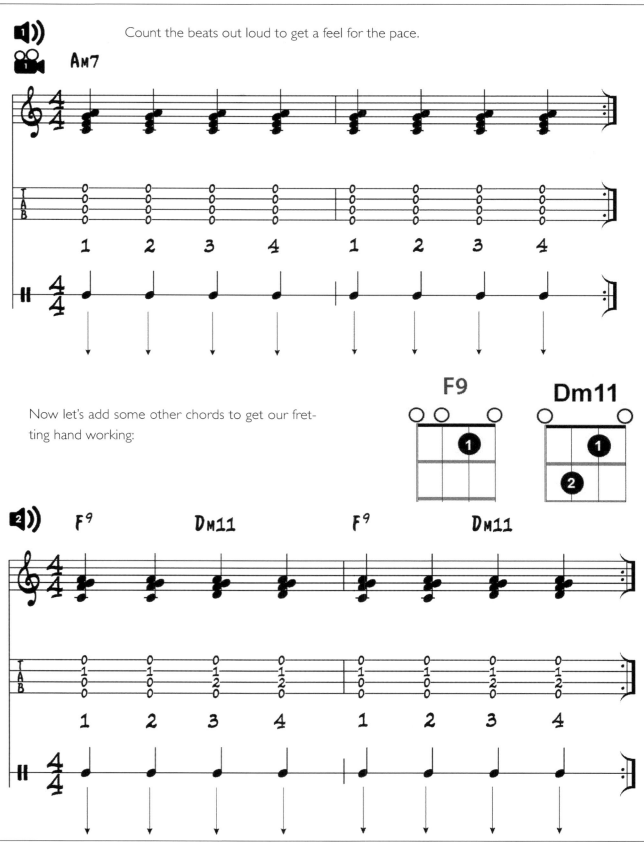

In the last example, the 1st finger (the index finger of your fretting hand) is placed on the 1st fret of the E-string. The 2nd finger (the middle finger of your fretting hand) is placed on the 2nd fret of the C-string. Hold the first finger down throughout the whole exercise.

The next pattern forms the basis of most other strumming patterns. Instead of playing only down strokes, like in Strumming 1.a, we'll play alternate down and up strokes in eighth notes. Remember to use the nail of the index finger for down strokes and the nail of the thumb for up strokes.

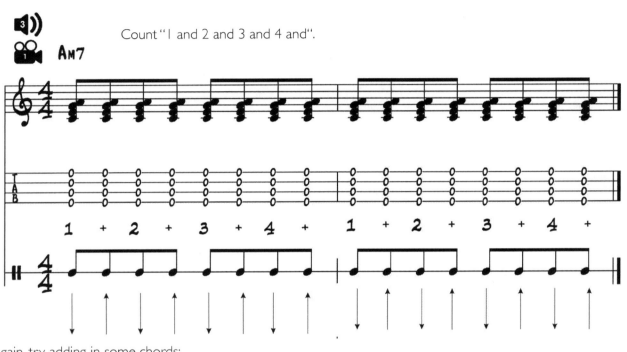

Again, try adding in some chords:

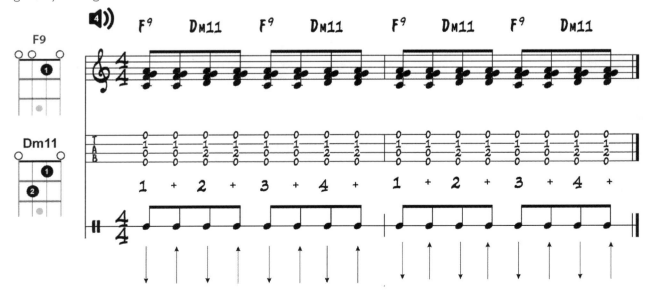

Now, lets combine the above pattern with an easy chord change

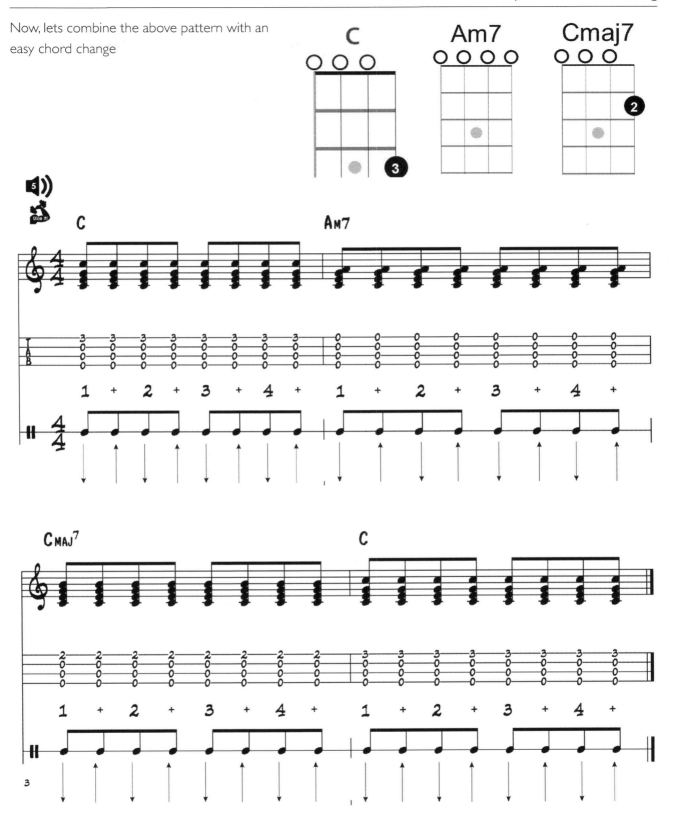

The last few examples had eight 1/8th notes in each bar. Almost all basic strumming patterns are constructed from a combination of 1/4 notes and 1/8th notes.

When strumming chords, always keep your strumming hand moving up and down all the time in even 1/8th notes, even if you are not making contact with the strings
This next section is all about learning rhythms. Chords are usually indicated above the pattern but if no chords are indicated simply use a C major chord:

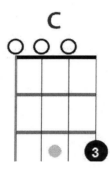

The next strumming pattern shows you one way to combine 1/4 notes and 1/8th notes. Remember to keep your strumming hand moving up and down in time throughout. A 1/4 note is played with a down strum, 1/8th notes are played with a "down up":

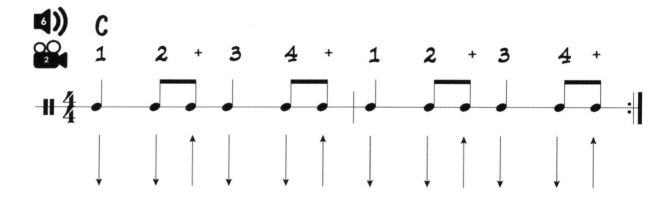

Count out loud with the audio track before attempting to play along with the ukulele.

> **Muting:**
> Mute the ukulele by placing your fretting hand gently across the strings and then repeat the strumming pattern above. With the muted 'scratch' sound you can hear the rhythm more clearly and focus only on the strumming hand. You can practice every strumming pattern with mute before adding chords later.

Chapter 1 - Basic Strumming

When you feel that you've mastered the last strumming pattern, add in the chords from audio example 5. If you feel like you occasionally lose the rhythm, keep returning to the audio example and play along.

Example 7 shows an important strumming pattern which is often used in popular songs.

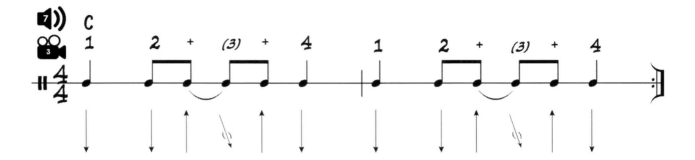

In this pattern, there is no strum on beat three: our strumming hand keeps moving, but we simply miss the strings on the down strum. The italic arrow indicates this "silent" strumming movement. Listen to the rhythm on the audio track. It helps you say the strumming pattern out loud " Down, Down up,   up Down."

Example 8 is similar to the example 7. The only difference is that on beat 4+ there is an additional up stroke.

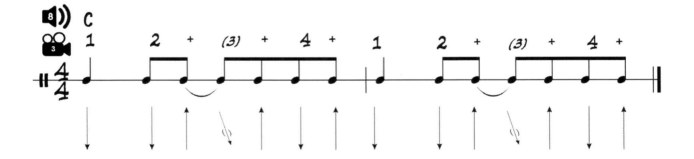

The previous two strumming patterns are interchangeable, and many players switch between them freely and unconsciously, depending on whether or not a chord change is occurring in the next bar. Often ukulele players skip the last 1/8th note of a bar if there's a chord change coming up. That way, they can create more time for an unnoticeable change.

Next, we will use the strumming patterns with different chord sequences. If you're having trouble with the notated chords, you can practice the chords first with an easier different strumming pattern like example 6 or example 1.

Chapter 1 - Basic Strumming

Use the same pattern and chords for **example 10.**

C   Am   F

🔊 10

C				Am			

4/4 / / / / | / / / / | / / / / | / / / /

F				C			

/ / / / | / / / / | / / / / | / / / / :||

Rotating Attentiveness - A Practicing Method

Our brain can only concentrate on a few things at a time. In order to have a good practice session, you should focus your attention on a different aspect of playing with each repetition.

You should always be attentive and focused while practicing. As soon as you notice that you are losing your concentration (after a concentrated phase), you should have a short break or concentrate on a different aspect. You can revise some of the other strumming patterns or play your favorite song just for fun, before you'll come back to the subject at hand.

Often it's best just to take a break and walk around.

Perfect practice is different for everybody and only you can observe yourself and draw conclusions. A practicing diary can be a very helpful tool to see your progress at a glance.

Find more information on practicing in Chapter 3.4 "Brain-optimized Practicing".

Many songs use a combination of the strummings in example 7/8 and example 6. This happens most often when a chord change occurs in the middle of a bar. **Example 11** shows you how it works.

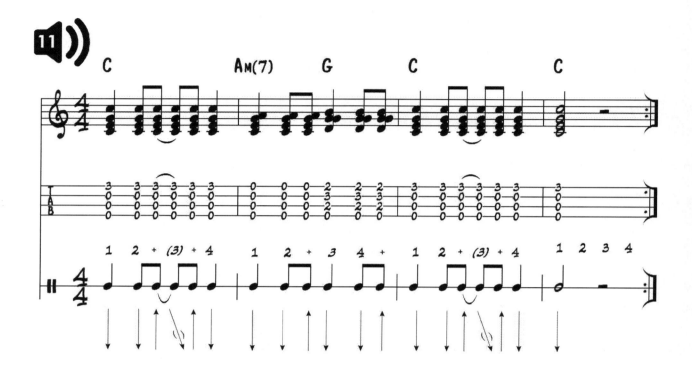

The notation can be simplified like this:

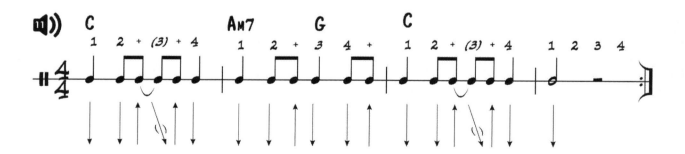

In the second bar there is a change from Am7 to G on beat 3. This Am7 chord gives your fingers a chance to prepare G chord. Try to place the three notes of the G chord on the fretboard simultaneously. This can be hard at first so take your time, go slowly, and be patient while practicing!

Chapter 1 - Basic Strumming

Find more information on chord types in *Pop & Rock Ukulele: Chords and Chord Structures*.

The following strumming patterns allow you to practice the chords of C, Am, F and G in different combinations. Repeat the examples as often as you can, and also play along with the audio tracks.

Example 12 is very similar to example 11. Try to play smoothly without pauses:

 Repeat this chord progression to practice both the strumming patterns and the chord changes.

Sometimes we adjust the fingering of a chord to make the following chord easier to play. Use the 3rd finger to play C Major and the 1st finger to play A minor. The first finger can then be shifted across a string to form the bottom note of the G Major chord.

25

Pop & Rock Ukulele

The following chord progressions are commonly used in pop music. Example 13, is built around the important "1 6 4 5" chord sequence in the key of C Major. You can learn more about music theory and chords in my book *Pop & Rock Ukulele: Chords and Chord Structures*.

On page <Ref> I've included a list of songs that you can play with this chord progression.

Example 14 is another chord progression that is frequently used in pop; the "1 5 6 4".

Some songs that use this chord progression are listed also on page <ref>. These chords are important because you can play many pop songs with a combination of just these four chords.

 A great exercise is to try is to work out a song's chord progression just by listening and trying out different chords.

My book *Pop & Rock Ukulele: Chords and Chord Structure* shows you ways to change keys (transposing) and how to move chords around the fretboard so you can alter them or construct them from scratch.

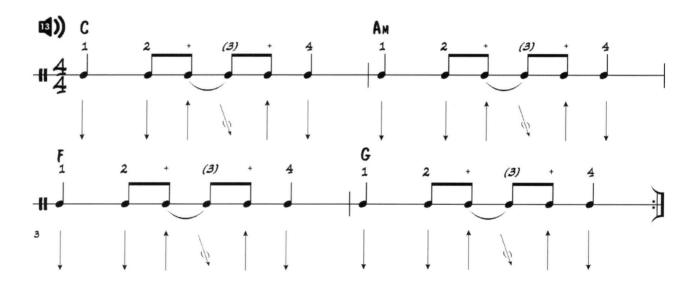

And a bit easier to read:

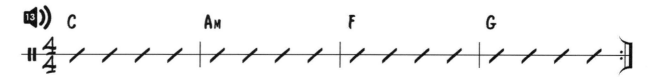

Chapter 1 - Basic Strumming

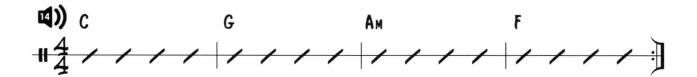

In this example, it is best to use the 2nd finger for the Am chord because it leaves the 1st finger free to play the F chord.

Example 14 speeds things up:

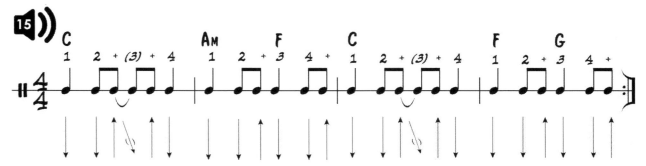

Now combine the two strumming patterns on your own:

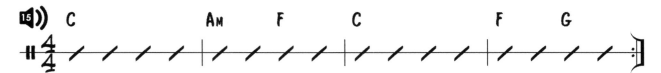

Here's an example of the "1 6 4 5" chord progression in a faster harmonic rhythm:

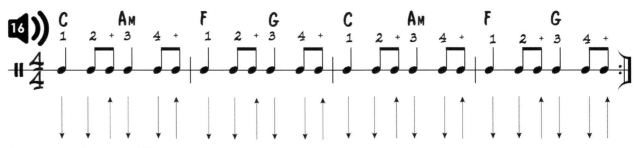

Also commonly notated like this:

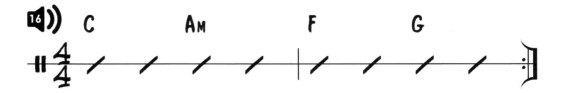

Famous songs listed by chord progressions:

1 6 4 5

C Am F G in the key of C Major
G Em C D in the key of G Major

- Bruno Mars – Just the way you are
- Dj Ötzi – Hey Baby
- Elton John – Crocodile Rock
- Ronald & Ruby- Lollipop
- Ben E. King – Stand by me
- The Marcels – Blue Moon
- The Marvelettes – Please Mr. Postman
- Chubby Checker – Let's Twist again

1 5 6 4
„Four Chord Songs"

C G Am F in the key of C Major
G D Em C in the key of G Major

- Bob Marley – No Woman No Cry
- Jason Mraz – I'm Yours
- Green Day – When I come around
- James Blunt – You're beautiful
- Akon – Don't matter
- John Denver – Take me home, country roads
- Elton John – Can you feel the love tonight

Of course, there are many more songs that use these chord progressions. If you listen to pop music carefully, you'll be able to hear these chord progressions occurring over and over again

After working through the previous examples you can now build the two bar strumming pattern used by Four Non-Blondes in the song "What's Up". In **example 17** I play the original chord progression twice in G major.

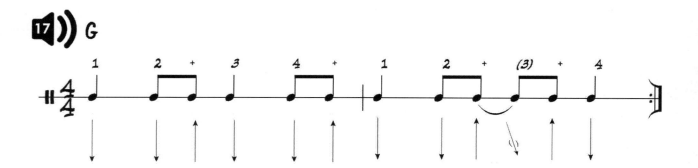

Chapter 1 - Basic Strumming

The chord progression of the song is repeated throughout. |: G – Am – C – G:|.

Each chord is held for two bars.

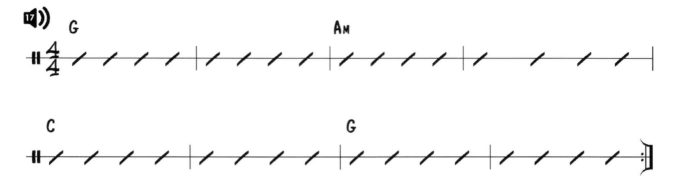

The original recording of the song is in G# major, one half-step up.

The next example shows a popular strumming variation used in the second bar.

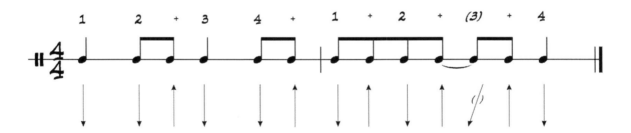

You can hear the variation in **example 18.**

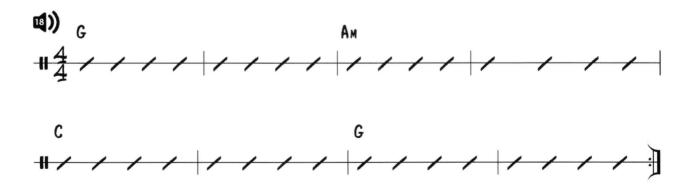

Listen carefully to the audio tracks to hear the difference between these patterns.

29

MODULES FOR NEW PATTERNS IN 4/4

Some other options you can use as rhythmic fills are shown in the following examples.

Each bar is played twice in the audio track. There are more strumming patterns available on our Facebook and Twitter pages. Follow us on Facebook and Twitter to find them.

www.facebook.com/poprockukuklele
www.twitter.com/poprockukulele

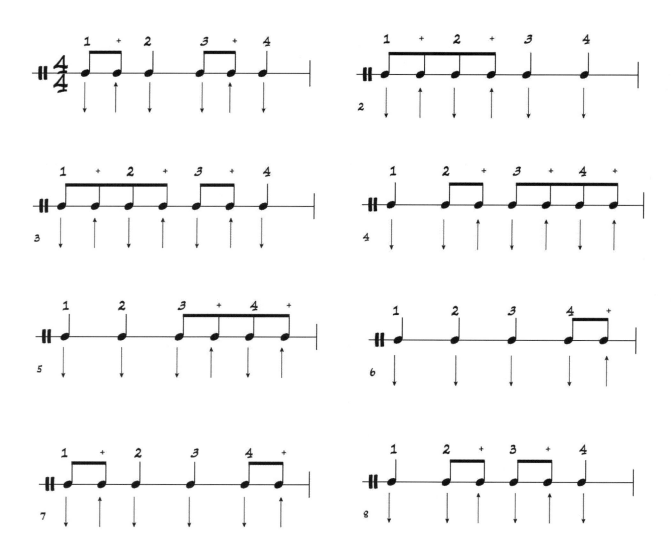

Chapter 1 - Basic Strumming

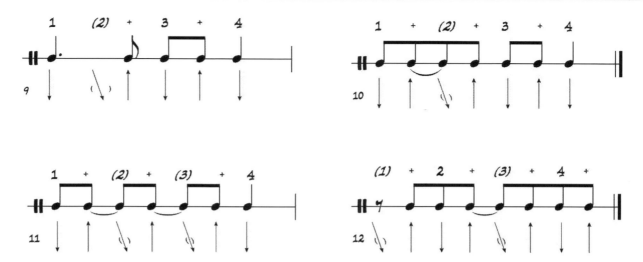

Until now, we've played each strumming pattern with a "straight" feel. This means that all the 1/8th notes were the same length. However, you can also play 1/8th notes with a "Shuffle" or "Swing" feel.

SWING PATTERNS

When playing with a shuffle feel, each 1/4 note is divided into three equal parts.

In a shuffle, the first two notes of each three are tied together to create the following rhythm:

Instead of writing out this complicated notation shuffle feels are often shown by the sign:

31

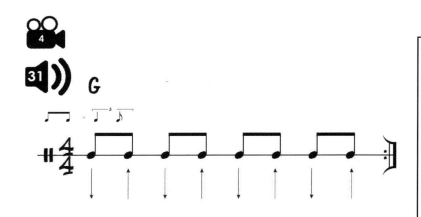

This sign is telling us that each 1/8th note should be played as a triplet rhythm. Listen to **example 31** to hear how this should sound.

Finally, here is a "straight" strumming pattern, that is often used in slow ballads. It starts simply, but more movement shortly before the end of the bar:

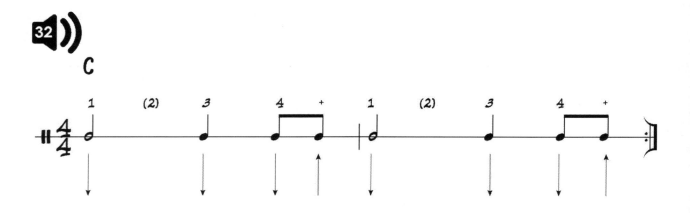

The audio download includes backing tracks without the ukulele to help you practice all the strumming ideas and feels in the book. It's like having your own virtual drummer! Head over to www.fundamental-changes.com to download the audio files now.

Chapter 1 - Basic Strumming

STRUMMING IN 3/4

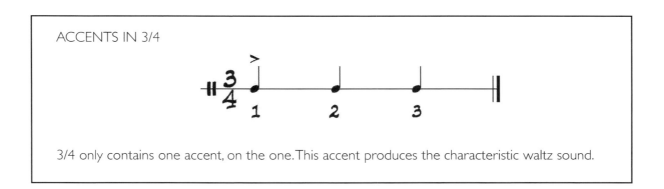

ACCENTS IN 3/4

3/4 only contains one accent, on the one. This accent produces the characteristic waltz sound.

A bar of 3/4 contains three 1/4 notes. The strumming patterns are constructed in the same way as in 4/4, but the feel of the music is totally different.

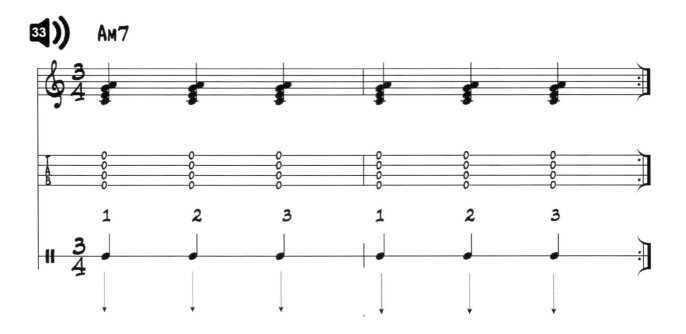

Just as in the previous chapter, we can replace any 1/4 note with two 1/8th notes and create new strumming patterns that way.

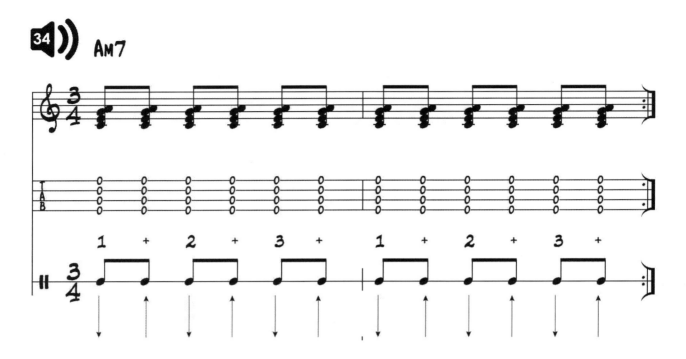

A very common 3/4 pattern is shown in **example 35.**

Chapter 1 - Basic Strumming

MODULES FOR NEW PATTERNS IN 3/4

The following tracks are all played with a C Major chord.

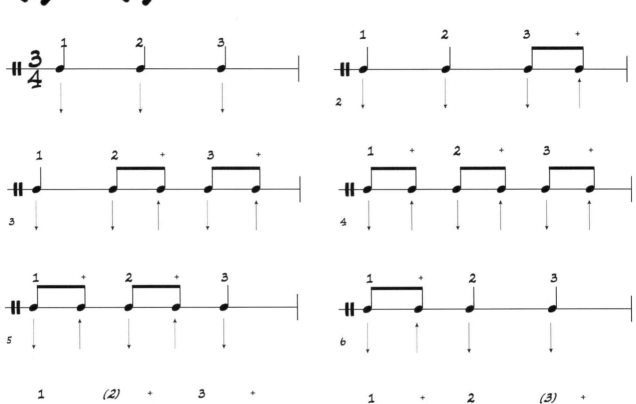

The following chords are needed to play the piece of music, **"Dancing Morning Sun"**.
Work through them carefully before learning the piece.

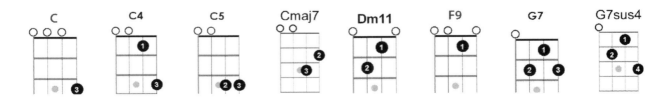

Dancing Morning Sun

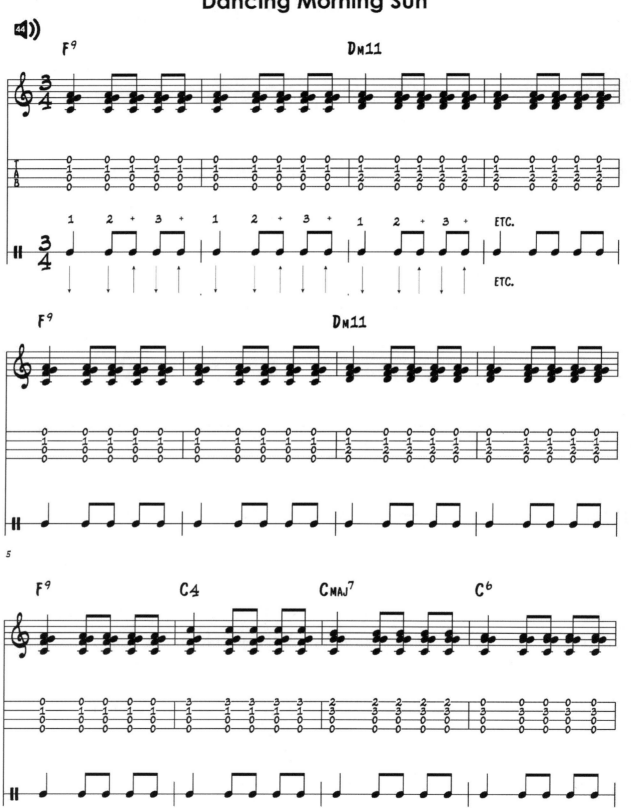

STRUMMING IN 6/8

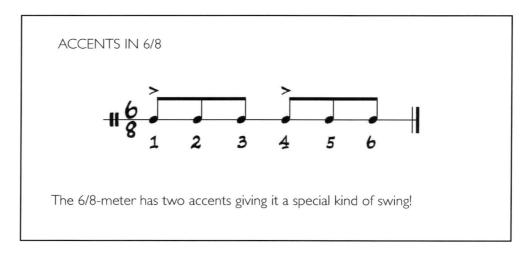

In theory you'll find the same number of 1/8th notes in a bar of 6/8, as in a bar a the 3/4. However, they are stressed differently, giving the music a very different feel.

6/8 tends to have a wonderful dance feel at fast tempos so the audio examples are quite quick. If they're too fast for you, read "Practicing with a Metronome" chapter and start at a tempo that is right for you.

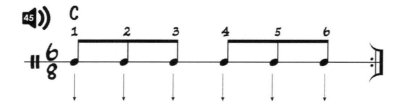

Just as a 1/4 note can be divided into 1/8th notes, one 1/8th note can be divided up into two 1/16th notes.

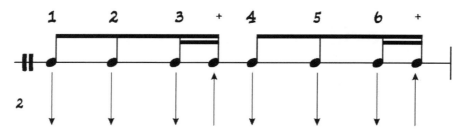

By 'doubling up' on an 1/8th note we can create the different patterns that you see below.

Chapter 1 - Basic Strumming

You may look at the examples below and wonder what the difference is between two bars of 3/4 and one bar of 6/8. The answer lies in the natural accents that we discussed earlier. In a bar of 3/4 there are three even beats that are divided into groups of two. In 6/8 there are two even beats that are divided into groups of three.

Most nursery rhythms are written in 6/8. Say out loud, 'Hickory Dickory Hickory Dickory', and then with the same rhythm say, '**1** 2 3 **4** 5 6 **1** 2 3 **4** 5 6'. Accent the 1 and 4 and you're talking in 6/8!

In 3/4, you would say '**1** & **2** & **3** & **1** & **2** & **3** &' to create three even beats that are divided into groups of two.

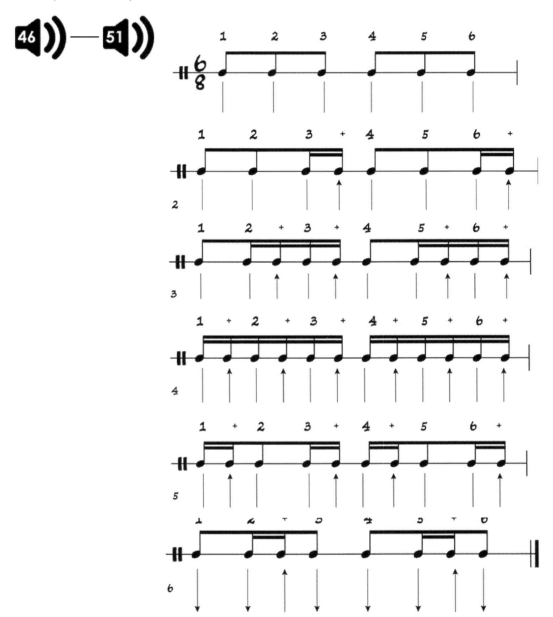

"We are the Champions" by Queen and "House of the Rising Sun" by the Animals are among the most famous rock songs in 6/8. Listen to these songs and try to count along with them "1 2 3 4 5 6". You'll find many different versions, especially of "House of the Rising Sun".

Chapter 2 - Advanced Strumming

This chapter introduces some more advanced strumming techniques such as 1/16th note rhythms and percussive mutes. While the strumming hand is very important, the fretting hand has a huge influence on many percussive elements in your playing. The fretting hand can mute the strings and add to the rhythm and texture of the pattern. To create a percussive muting sound it is useful to use a barre chord. You can read more detailed advice about barre chords and their techniques in the Technique Kit in Chapter 3.

1/16TH NOTE STRUMMING

In 4/4, 1/8th notes were the smallest rhythmical unit. Go back and look at the basic 1/8th note patterns you'll notice that 1/8th notes are normally grouped in pairs. The first 1/8th note is played with a down stroke while the second 1/8th note is played with an up stroke. This alternate strumming idea applies to 1/16th notes too. It looks like this:

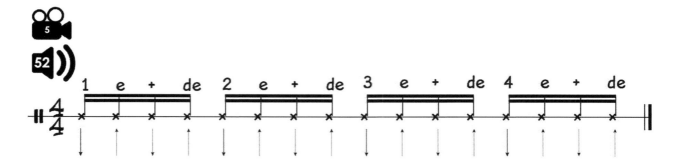

Each 1/4 note is divided into a group of four 1/16th notes.
Play the following examples using this barre chord:

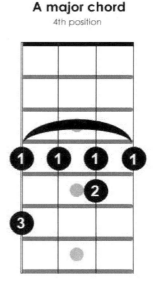

A major chord
4th position

Begin by placing your fingers on the strings with a tiny amount of pressure so that you're just touching the strings, but not pressing them down against the frets.

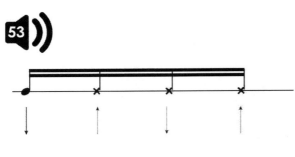

In **example 53** the first 1/16th of the group is sounding while the other three strums are muted. These muted notes are called "Dead notes" and they are created by placing the fingers on the strings without applying enough pressure to sound an actual pitch. To allow the un-muted strum to ring out, simply squeeze the fretting hand fingers and push the strings against the fret.

Listen to the audio track, watch the video and repeat the rhythm to get a feeling for when to "squeeze" and when to relax.
In Chapter 3, you'll find a great tapping exercise that is helpful for practicing this technique.

There are many different ways to combine muted notes and full chords. In the next example the *first* two 1/16th notes are muted and the third 1/16th is sounding to create a Reggae feel.

Now combine the two previous groups into one bar.

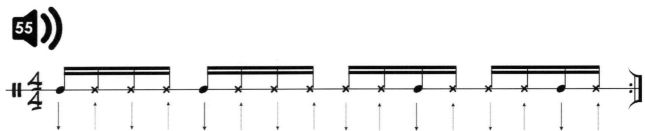

This is repeated four times on the audio track.

Chapter 2 - Advanced Strumming

Unmuted chords can also be placed on *unaccented* 1/16th notes. You can see this in the next few strumming patterns.

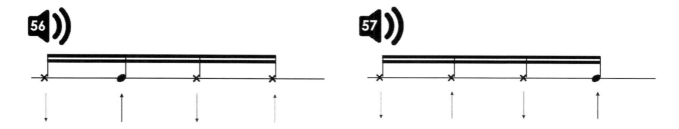

It is important to learn to rhythmically place any strum where you want it to sound, but it is also important to learn to accent any strum you wish. Example 58 is a good exercise to develop this control. Focus on where the unmuted notes are played. The alternate between up- and down-strokes.

Example 58 is notated in 12/16, so every sounding note falls onto a naturally accented spot in the bar.

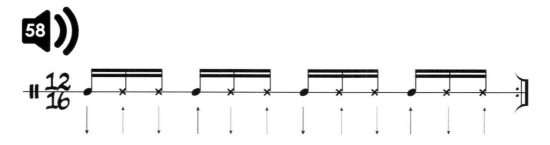

Let's incorporate this rhythmic element in a full 4/4 strumming pattern:

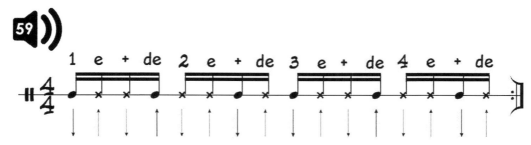

You could also notate the pattern like this to make the rhythmic groupings more visible:

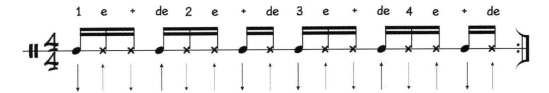

The bar is divided into two groups of 3 and one group of 2. You'll learn this rhythm most quickly by saying it out loud. When you say "**Pa**-na-ma-**Pa**-na-ma-**Cu**-ba-**Pa**-na-ma-**Pa**-na-ma-**Cu**-ba" without a break, you create the same rhythm. Try to speak along with the audio track and listen carefully to the audio track.

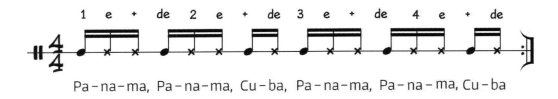

Look at the collection of rhythmic fragments below. They teach you different ways to divide up a group of 1/16ths. Create different combinations and practice them slowly at first before gradually increase the speed.

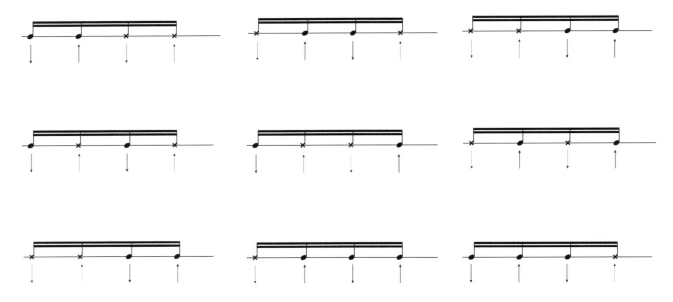

Example 60 is a Funk riff that uses some of these combinations:

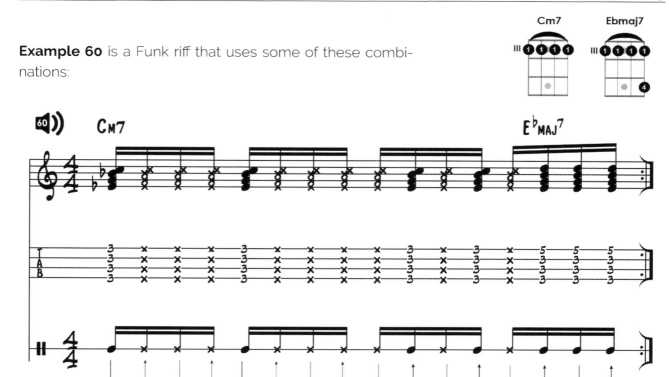

Example 61 is similar, yet forms from a very different pattern using a moving barre chord.

In order to be able to move the barre chord cleanly, you'll need a stable position for yourself and your ukulele so that your fretting hand can move easily.

Go to the appendix to find out how to develop a stable position for yourself and the ukulele.

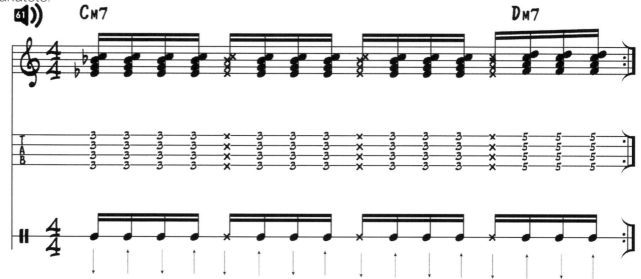

FLAMENCO TECHNIQUES

Spanish Flamenco is famous for its complex strumming techniques which are performed not just with the index finger and the thumb, but the whole hand.

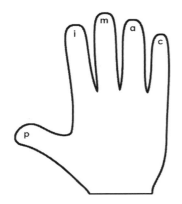

The fingers of the strumming hand have the following names:
These labels derive from the Spanish words for the single fingers (**p**ulgar, **i**ndice, **m**edio, **a**nular and **c**hico).

p = thumb.
i = index finger.
m = for middle finger.
a = for ring finger.
c = for pinky.

If you're new to flamenco techniques, I suggest that you begin by practicing without the ukulele. Study the following pictures carefully and follow the movements with your strumming fingers:

First Position Thumb

First Position Thenar

The images show how all four fingers are "squeezed" into the palm of your hand. You can either squeeze them behind the base of your thumb (thenar) as shown in the first image or you can squeeze them behind your thumb first to get a feel for the technique.

Let your fingers "burst" out one by one. This movement of each finger is fast, quick impulse, but without great force. Focus on feeling the muscles in the back of your hand.

When you succeed in creating this fast movement, you will hear the sound of your fingernails scraping over the skin of your palm.

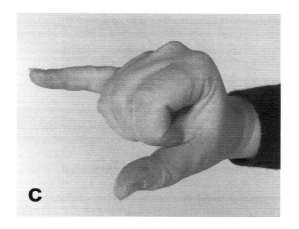

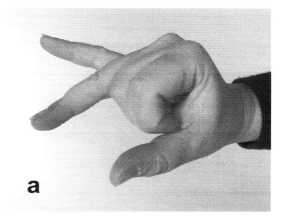

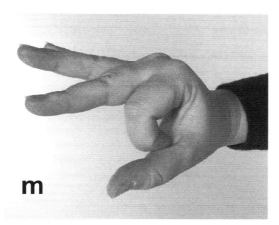

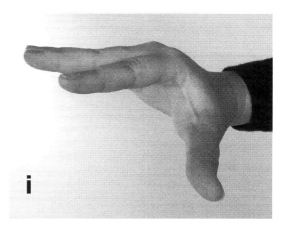

You can practice this sequential finger movement by using a piece of cardboard. Aim to hit the cardboard with your fingernails in sequence as shown in the image below:

After practicing this movement, you can now move it to the ukulele. At first, mute the strings with your fretting hand so that you can hear the rhythm clearly. You don't have to hit every string with every finger, but you should aim for hitting at least two strings each time.

The thumb stays up and doesn't rest on top of the ukulele or a string.

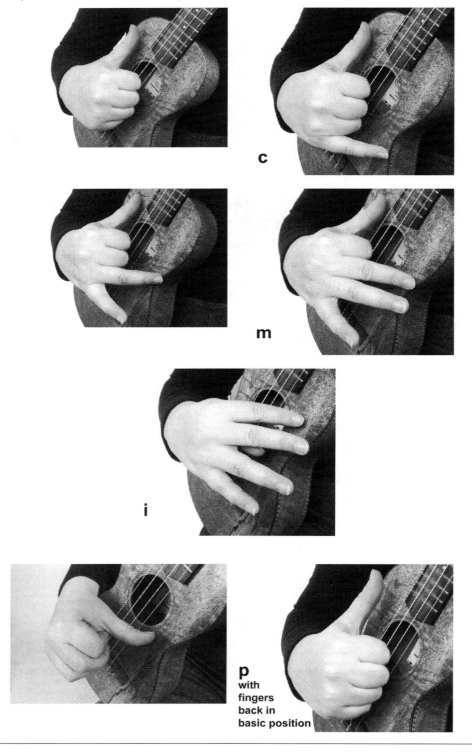

c

m

i

p
with fingers back in basic position

Chapter 2 - Advanced Strumming

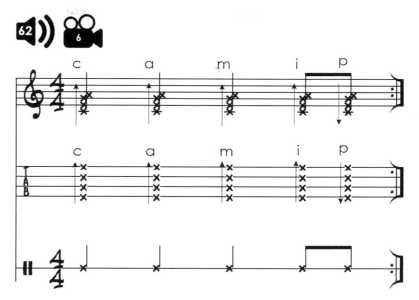

Mute the strings with your frettting hand.

Practice the same pattern, but now start with your index finger:

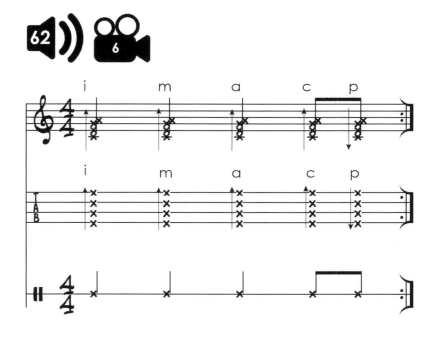

Be patient while practicing as your fingers will not all move with equal ease. Don't overdo it! Build your muscles slowly and surely.

Try to practice for a few short periods each day. You can practice while on the go by using the earlier practice exercises without the ukulele. If your muscles begin to hurt, take a break until your hand is relaxed again and your muscles have recovered. It is important to take breaks to avoid tendon strain.

Here is a flamenco pattern that I like to use:

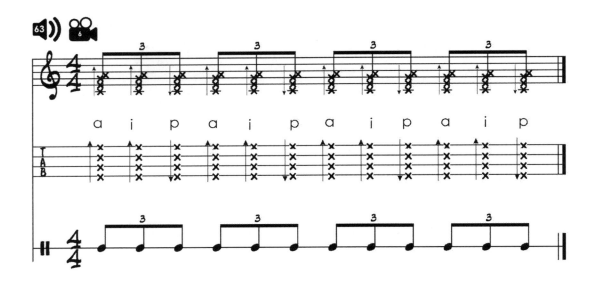

This one is a little more challenging:

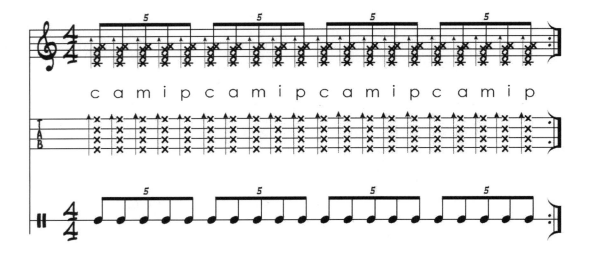

Chapter 2 - Advanced Strumming

STRUMMING WITH "SPECIAL EFFECTS"

Palm Mute - Muting with your strumming hand

We've already seen how we can mute strumming patterns with the fretting hand when using barre chords, however we can also mute with the palm of the strumming hand. This can be done while strumming or immediately afterwards.

With the ball of your thumb

With the heel of your hand

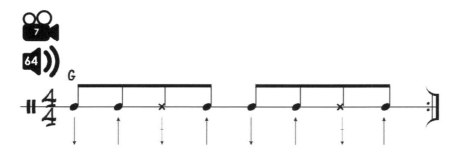

Experiment with the positioning of your strumming hand to create a gentle, yet firm muted sound. You can hear how this should sound on the following audio example.

Example 65 shows you how to incorporate this technique into example 7 from chapter 1.

Enhanced Strumming - Flamenco-influenced Patterns

You can spice up *Strumming pattern No. 7* (again G major) with an easy flamenco technique. The wavy arrow stands for flamenco strumming and the fingers to use are marked next to it.

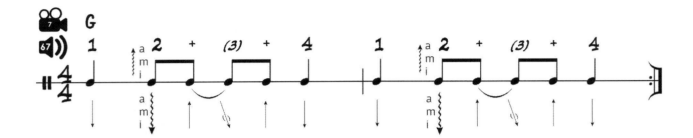

You can also use all four fingers when strumming the accentuated 'flamenco' beat (c a m i). This makes the accented beat even more elaborate.
Make sure to focus on rhythmic precision and listen to the audio tracks to hear how this should sound.

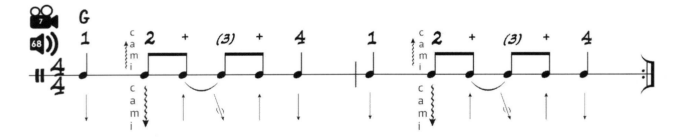

Strumming with Percussion

You can enrich any strumming pattern that you've learned so far by adding percussive sounds such as drumming or knocking on the uke. Don't be afraid that you might damage the instrument, as the body and top of your ukulele are strong.
One way to produce a "snare drum" sound is by slapping the strings with your open hand. The snare sound is produced by the strings hitting the frets on the fretboard.

Percussion with your hand

Chapter 2 - Advanced Strumming

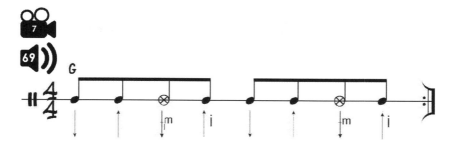

The symbol "m" (for lat. manus = hand) together with an arrow and the percussion sign indicates this "snare" hit with your open hand. Afterward the slap you play an upstroke with your index finger creating a soft sound on the off beat.

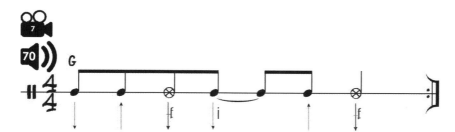

You can also hit with your fist (f, together with the arrow and the percussion sign).

Note that in this example you perform a down stroke after the hit!
Here, the natural order of up and down alternate strokes is broken as you place a down stroke on the up beat. This down stroke accents the usually unaccented up beat in the bar. The elongation of the note (tie) adds to the accented effect.
 You can play calm acoustic-ballads as well as rhythmical songs with the strumming pattern in *Example 70*. You'll find ideas for that in the next section.

When hitting the ukulele with your fist, you can also try to "miss" the instrument with the thumb and index finger, so you can immediately hit the top of the ukulele instead of the strings to create a more percussive sound. Don't worry! Your Ukulele can handle it!

Percussion with your fist

Index finger hitting the top

STRUMMING IN SONGS

In this section we look at the strumming patterns in two famous songs that are very popular on the ukulele.

You can use Example 70 to play "I'm yours" by Jason Mraz. The strumming pattern is played twice for each chord.

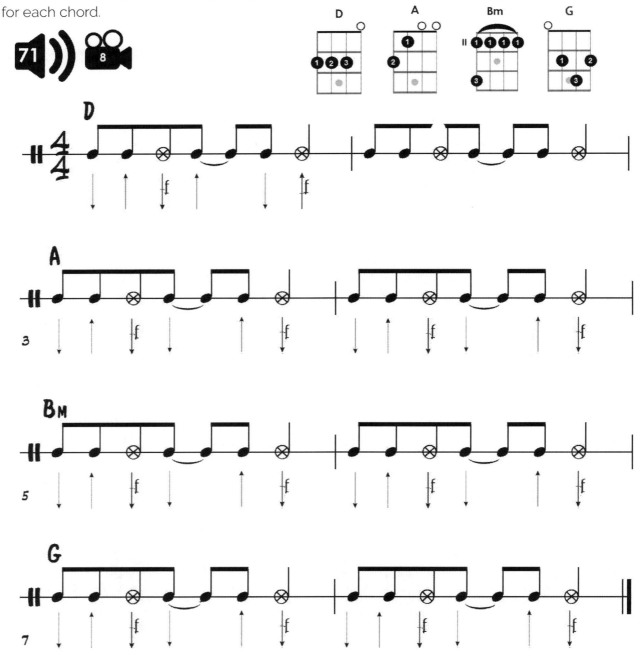

My book, Ukulele Chords and Chord Structures teaches you many different ways to voice these chords.

Chapter 2 - Advanced Strumming

Israel Kamakawiwo'ole has made a wonderful version "Somewhere over the Rainbow" on the ukulele. The strumming pattern is actually quite easy:

You can see that some arrows are bigger and bolder than others. These strums are played louder than the other strokes. Begin by practicing everything with the same dynamic before accenting the "big" strums later.

On the original recording, the strumming is quite fast and each strum is played with the index finger i. This will result in two different tone colors that give the pattern a very special dynamic.

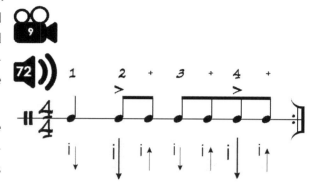

down

up

Am7 is played like this:

Am7

The intro for "Somewhere over the rainbow", uses these chords:

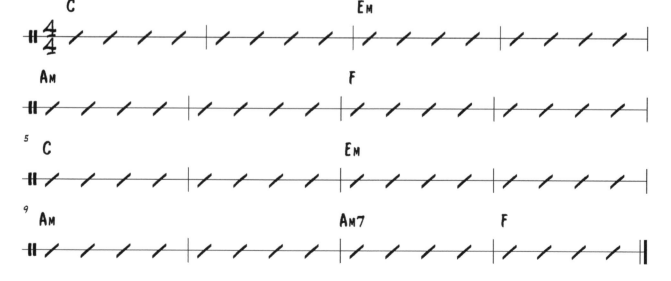

Each chord is played for two bars with the exception of the last two chords of the intro.

You don't always have to stick to the strumming pattern of the recorded version! Try out a number of different patterns to decide on what you like best. Try your best to capture the feel of a song when you play.

Chapter 3 – Technique Kit

In this section you'll find techniques and tips that help you to develop your strength and fluency and allow you to play with ease.

EXERCISES FOR YOUR FRETTING HAND

At first, it can be difficult to place your fingers properly on each note resulting in unpleasant sounds like buzzes and scratches.

Sometimes these buzzes occur because you're not pressing the string on the best spot. Each finger should be close to the relevant fret, but not on it. Correct placement is easy with one finger at the time, but when fretting chords, other fingers can sometimes get in the way. It's important to find a good position for every finger in the chord.

When fretting notes on the ukulele your fingers can approach the fretboard in two directions. The first approach is to place your fingers parallel to the fret wire. This can be a great approach for some chords but this position might make fretting difficult for others.

The other way of approaching the fretboard is "from above". With this method, the fingers approach the frets coming in at an angle from the headstock. Both ways have advantages and disadvantages however most people find that a combination of the two approaches will enable them to play any chord. It'll be your job to try out which way works better for you.

Look at the pictures below to see the difference in these approaches.

You can see, that the fingers in the G chord are close to the frets. Especially the index finger looks like it's coming in from the headstock of the uke, from "above". Compared to the "parallel" approach this creates a lot more space for the 2nd finger.

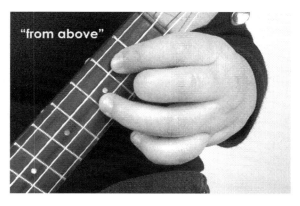

For the F chord shown in the following pictures, it might be more comfortable to try a "parallel" approach to create more space for the 1st finger.

Each chord's hand-position can be different, depending on the situation. Sometimes "parallel" is better than "from above". Try to find the appropriate position (which can be different from player to player) for every chord, and don't be afraid to change your approach if you realize that a different position would be more effective.

There are three main reasons for buzzing:

- Not pressing hard enough
- Pressing the wrong spot, causing slight muting or buzzing in other strings
- Not pressing close enough to the fret.

For most ukuleles you don't need a lot of force when you press down the strings so buzzing is usually the result of pressing the wrong spot. As there is no method that works for every player; I'm afraid you'll need a little bit of patience to find your own best position.

Play through each note in the chord one by one to find the note that needs adjusting

Chapter 3 - Technique Kit

Tapping exercise

This exercise has been very helpful to me and my students throughout my years teaching guitar. It may appear simple at first, but it has a wonderful, relaxing effect on the fingers. This "silent" exercise teaches your fingers to move independently, without having to worry about producing a perfect note.

Place your fingers in the "Four-Finger-Position". In other words, place the four fingers of your fretting hand on the same string, one finger per fret.

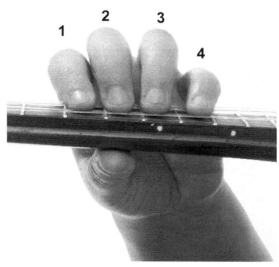

Take it in turns to tap each finger onto its allocated fret. Imagine that the finger is "falling" against the fretboard. You may hear a sound, but it will most likely be silent. The exercise is about leading the finger (in a relaxed manner) to its position on the fretboard.

You'll get a feel for the individual movements of your fingers. Apply the same number of repetitions to each finger by counting to eight while tapping.

In the photo, you can see that the thumb is placed across from the middle finger. This fixes your hand in position, but the thumb shouldn't press too firmly against the fretboard.

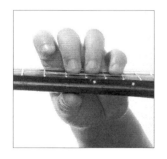   

This exercise has a few benefits:

- It relaxes the muscles in your hand, by gently repeating the same movement a few times in a row.
- It teaches you to guide the finger back to the same spot on the fretboard.
- It teaches you to fret with your fingertip.

In Chapter 3.4 you can read about "Rotating Attentiveness". With this practicing method you can concentrate on one of the aspects above at a time.

Pop & Rock Ukulele

CHORDS

Chord Diagrams

Chords are usually depicted in chord diagrams which show the strings, frets and where the fingers need to be placed.
All chord diagrams in this book are for standard tuning ukulele: G-C-E-A.

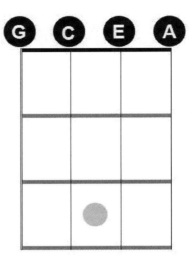

The fingers of the fretting hand are called:

Index finger = finger 1
Middle finger = finger 2
Ring finger = finger 3
Pinky = finger 4

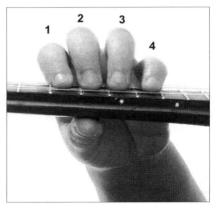

The following diagram shows the chord of A Major. Notice, finger numbers are indicated on each note. The following chord uses just the 1st and 2nd finger.

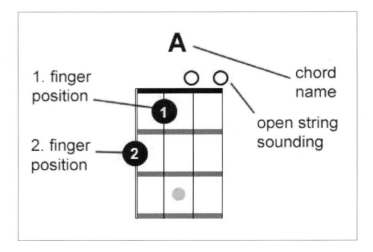

60

Chapter 3 - Technique Kit

Chords in 1st position

Fretting positions on the ukulele are identified by finger 1 (the index finger) of your fretting hand. 1st position is defined by the finger 1 being placed on the first fret of your ukulele.

The other fingers fret accordingly. That means that the index finger frets the first fret, while middle finger, ring finger and pinky each fret the second, third and fourth fret.

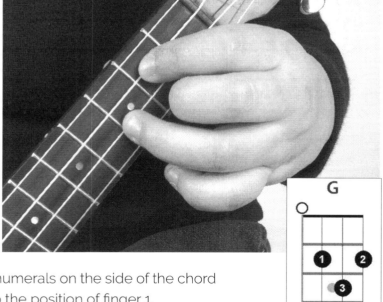

Let's have a look at the F chord. You can see that finger 1 frets the first fret, while finger 2 frets the second fret.

This method works great for scales and melodies, but doesn't always hold up for chords. If you look at the chord diagram and picture below, you'll find that the 1st finger frets the second fret, while the middle finger and the ring finger each fret their first position frets.

Some people like to identify positions by the positions of finger 2 or the majority of fingers.

Other positions are indicated by roman numerals on the side of the chord diagram. These numbers always refer to the position of finger 1.

This is a collection of the most important chords in the 1st position. I've used the most common keys, so you can play lots of popular songs. I've included common fingering alternatives for some chords.

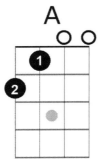
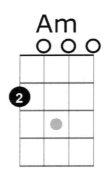
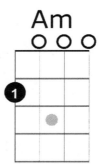
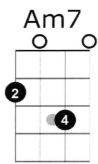

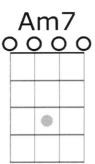
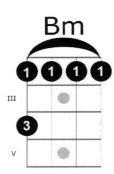
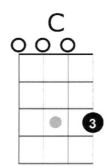
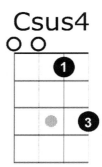

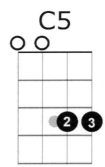
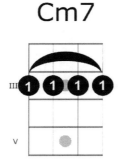
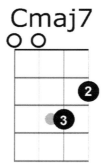
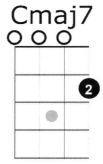

Take time to find a good position for the thumb. Look at the pictures in chapter 3.1 and compare them with your own hand. This will reduce problems with the fretting hand and enable you to play for longer periods of time.

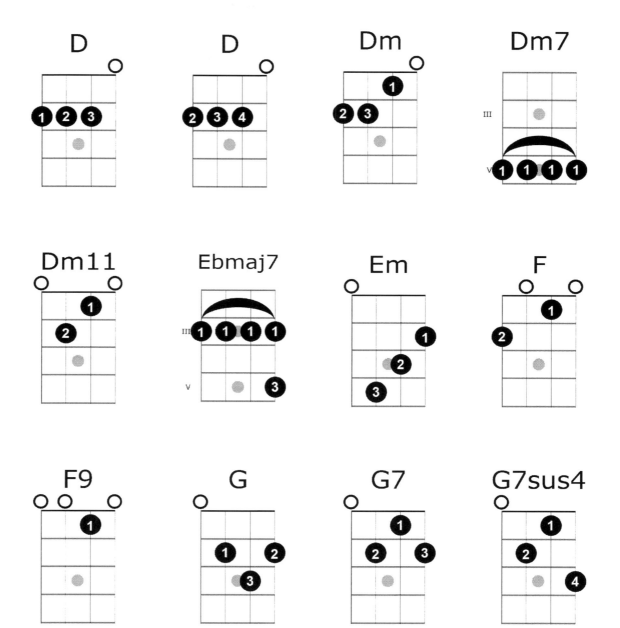

Barre chords

Barre chords are chords where one finger is used to fret more than one string. This can be notated in the following ways:

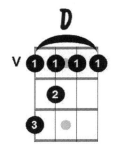 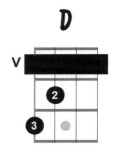

I've chosen the first version for "Pop & Rock Ukulele".

Barre chords are usually played with your 1st finger (although other fingers can be used).

Like all techniques, mastering barre chords is different for everybody. You'll have to find the position that works best for you. As long as your position is relatively relaxed and doesn't constrain other techniques, it's the right one for you. Feel free to arrive at different results than me.

The area you use for fretting lies diagonally on the side of the finger, right where the creases in your fingers end and you can feel the bone. Don't fret too heavily with the side of the finger as you'll start to encounter restriction in your other fingers.

Chapter 3 - Technique Kit

Frequent mistakes:

Wrong side of the finger.

Finger frets too much on the side; the other fingers can't fret in a relaxed fashion.

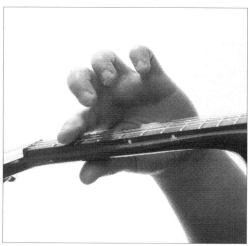

Finger is too high on the fretboard causes fretting too close to the hand joint.

When practicing barre chords make sure to take frequent breaks to relax your fretting hand.

65

Pop & Rock Ukulele

PRACTICING WITH A METRONOME

The audio tracks that accompany this book are, in most cases, available at two different tempos. However, you may not be able to reach your musical goals with the audio tracks alone. The recording may be too fast for you, or you may need more practice at a lower speed.
The solution is to practice with a metronome allowing you to practice the strumming patterns at any tempo. It's important that you listen very carefully to the metronome and try to play exactly on its beat. This can be challenging.
There are different types of metronomes:

- **Classic Metronomes** are usually a pyramid shape and have a pendulum that swings one side to side to produce the click. You move a weight on the pendulum to make the pendulum swing at different speeds. Those metronomes look great but there are some disadvantages to them. They're not very handy and they only offer certain tempos.

- **Electronic Metronomes** have the advantage that they are usually practical and easy to transport. You can also adjust the tempos in steps of one beat per minute. Very often, you can also "tap in" the tempo you like and the metronome will continue the speed at which you were tapping.
  Usually you can set the first beat in a bar to make a different sound to the other clicks. Electronic Metronomes often allow you to set rhythmical subdivisions, like triplets, quintuplets or dotted notes. You can sometimes even program several features, such as playing different parts in different meters. These metronomes are often very expensive.
  Some electronic metronomes have an annoying electronic sound. You should test your metronome in the shop to determine whether you'll be able to practice with it, or not.

- **Apps:** If you don't want to invest in a metronome, you'll find different Smartphone Apps, like "Mobile Metronome" or "Metronome Beats" that are usually free and offer many useful features.
  The next step is to find the right tempo and learn how to practice well with it. The slower audio tracks have a tempo of 87bpm. That means, that 87 1/4 note beats sound every minute.

The next step is to find the right tempo and learn how to practice well with it.
The slower audio tracks have a tempo of 87bpm. That means, that 87 1/4 note beats sound every minute.
Musicians write this: ♩ = 87

Chapter 3 - Technique Kit

The fast audio tracks are recorded ♩ = 120 ("1/4 note equals 120").

If you can play along with the slower recordings quite well, but the fast recordings are too fast for you, you can increase the tempo step by step using the metronome. Count out loud with the metronome to get a feel for the tempo before you play the strumming pattern with the click.
Advanced players can try to 'hear' the strumming pattern in the tempo of the metronome before playing.

The metronome is a great tool for practicing if you use it consciously and purposefully.
Depending on the pattern, raise the tempo in small or big steps. Especially for patterns based on 1/16th notes the steps will be quite small. Don't advance too fast and be patient while practicing. Playing with speed takes time to develop.

Here's an example showing what a 'speeding up' practice session with a metronome might look like:

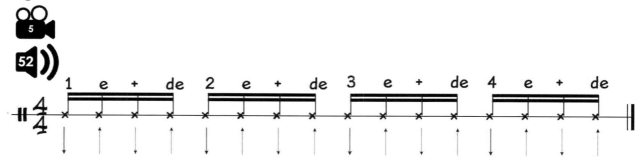

- Listen to audio example No. 52. It's record ♩ in = 87, which may seem quite fast.
- If it's too fast for you, set the metronome ♩ = 60 and try to play one group of 1/16ths between the beats. (To check for accuracy, set the metronome to 120 and make sure your down beats are on the beat of the metronome).
- Once you've mastered that speed, set the metronome a bit higher. Probably 65 is enough to give you a significant increase in speed.
- Work your way up to 87 by setting the metronome higher each time you've mastered the speed.
- Once you've reached 87 play along with the audio.
- When you've mastered it work to reach 120.
- At the end of the session write down your maximum speed so you remember it for the next session
- In your next session, you'll probably have to start a bit slower than your maximum speed and work up it before exceeding it

You'll have to work on your speed over the course of time.
Always stay relaxed.

BRAIN-OPTIMIZED PRACTICING

The subject of how to practice would easily fill more than one book as it such a diverse topic.

Top requirements for successful practicing are:

- Concentration
- Motivation
- Fitness (physical & mental)

Setting practice goals, concentrated practice time and incorporating breaks can enhance your focus and make you mentally and physically fitter. Motivation soon follows!

One of the most important practicing methods is „**Rotating Attentiveness**".

Our brain can only concentrate on a few things at a time. In order to have a good practice session, you should focus your attention on a different aspect of playing with each repetition.

You should always be attentive and focused while practicing. As soon as you notice that you are losing your concentration (after a concentrated phase), you should have a short break or concentrate on a different aspect. You can revise some of the other strumming patterns or play your favorite song just for fun, before you'll come back to the subject at hand.

Often it's best just to take a break and walk around.

Perfect practice is different for everybody and only you can observe yourself and draw conclusions. A practicing diary can be a very helpful tool to see your progress at a glance.

Recent studies have shown that the thing that influences your practicing results most is the ratio between successful and unsuccessful attempts. That means if you play a pattern 100 times, but you get it wrong 50 times out of those 100 attempts results showed to be worse than if you only played it 50 times but got it right every time.

So, concentrate, choose a speed where you can get it right immediately and practice more often but for shorter periods so that you are fresh and effective when you practice

Appendix

WHICH UKULELE?

As well as the "standard" ukulele, there are also soprano, concert, tenor and baritone ukuleles. All of them, except for the baritone are tuned in the standard tuning GCEA. The sizes of the ukulele are indicated in scale lengths, the same as on all other stringed instruments. The scale length is the length of the actual sounding string from the saddle to the bridge of the ukulele. The soprano ukulele is the smallest and has a scale length of just 33cm. The majority of ukuleles that you'll see in music shops are soprano ukuleles. Along with "standard" tuning (GCEA) the A D F#G tuning is also sometimes used on the soprano ukulele.

The concert ukulele has a scale length of 38cm and is sometimes tuned in "Low G". This means that the G-string is tuned one octave lower and replaced with a metal-wrapped nylon string.

The tenor ukulele is often the most comfortable ukulele for guitarists. It has a scale length of 43cm and is therefore quite a bit bigger than the soprano ukulele and produces a "bigger" sound. Many soloists, like Jake Shimabukuro play tenor ukuleles in concert. Standard tuning and "Low G" are the most common tunings, but sometimes they are tuned to D G B E, which corresponds with the top four strings of the guitar. However, the D string sounds an octave higher than the guitar.

The baritone ukulele has a scale length of 48cm and feels closest to the guitar. Usually it is tuned D G B E. Unlike other ukuleles, the strings of the baritone are tuned in from low to high, meaning that the D string is the lowest sounding and the E string the highest sounding string.

The number of accessible frets on your ukulele is important. At the moment I play a concert ukulele with 15 frets (most soprano ukuleles only have 12 or 13), and another with 19 frets. These all get used in performance.

When you buy a ukulele, you should ask yourself the following questions:

- What kind of music do I want to play on the ukulele
    - "Just" chords or solo repertoire, as well?
- What do I want to learn after the basics?
    - ◇ Improvising?
    - ◇ Chords in higher positions?
    - Solo repertoire?

The more advanced the pieces you want to play, the better your instrument should be. Quality is mainly reflected in the sound, but quality instruments are usually also easier to play, enabling you to master more difficult techniques.

Try out different instruments and take time to actually play the instrument in the shop. If you know a teacher, ask him or her to accompany you and help you to pick an instrument.

Test your prospective ukulele for buzzing or dead notes: all notes should ring clearly at each fret. If it is not possible to play easy chords, or if the notes in higher positions sound bad, it is probably better to invest a little bit more in a good instrument.

Pop & Rock Ukulele

A good instrument for beginners should have "proper fretting" (read below about what that is and how you can test it). Proper fretting is crucial for tuning the ukulele properly. The string action (height of the strings above the frets) shouldn't be too high allowing you to play easily in higher positions. If you get the right instrument you'll definitely be happy with your ukulele.

Of course, when you're getting better, the demands you make on your instrument will change with your abilities.

DIFFERENT WAYS OF TUNING

We've already mentioned that the "standard" tuning of the ukulele is to the notes G C E A although some books and songs use different tunings. Watch out when you buy music and books! - Make sure, they're for the right tuning for your ukulele!

The intervals between the strings are usually the same in all tunings and the intervals between the C E and A strings correspond directly with the intervals between the treble strings of the guitar. This means that you can apply music that is played on the treble strings of the guitar directly to the ukulele, although they will sound in a different key.

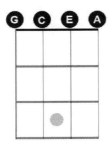

Tuning - Standard Tuning

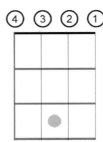

The strings of the ukulele are numbered as 1, 2, 3, 4, beginning with the A string.

You can memorize the order of the strings with the following sentence:

All **E**lephants **C**an **G**row

Comparing Unisons

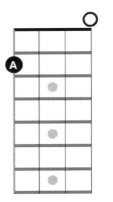
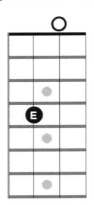
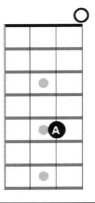

'Unisons' are two identical notes sounding together. By comparing the same note on different strings, you can tune your ukulele. You just have to "define" one string as being "in tune" and work from there.

Appendix

If we assume that the G string is in tune and play the note 'A' on the G string this should sound the same as the open A string. This way, we can compare if the open string sounds higher or lower than the fretted A note. Adjust the tuning of the open string until both notes sound identical.

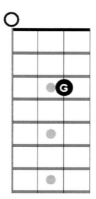

The next step is to play the open A string, (which is now in tune) and compare it to the note 'A' on the E string.

The C string is tuned in the same way. Again, pluck the open string, that you tuned last and compare it to the same note on another string.

You should also compare the E string to the G string, just to be sure.

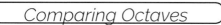
Comparing Octaves

Another tuning method for some strings is to "compare octaves". You can hear if a string is in tune by using octaves in a similar way to comparing unisons. An octave that is in perfectly tune has no friction or "tension" in its sound.

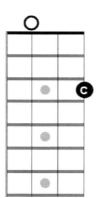
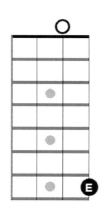

This method only works if your ukulele is properly fretted.

Use a combination of octaves and unisons when tuning your ukulele.

Is my Ukulele Properly Fretted?

When all the frets on a ukulele are placed correctly the notes they produce are in tune. You can check with a tuner to see if this is the case by using the octaves on each string or use one of the methods below.

The harmonic on the 12th fret should be the same pitch as the plucked note on the 12th fret. To play the harmonic put your finger exactly over the fret of the 12th fret, but don't push down. Pluck the string. If you're performing this technique correctly there will be a bell-like sound called a harmonic. When you play the "normal" note on the same fret (without the harmonic), there should be no difference in pitch.

When you place your finger on the string for the normally fretted note, make sure you do not pull or squeeze the string, as this will change the intonation and subsequently the pitch.

If the harmonic and the fretted 12th fret note do not match, it could a result of having old strings. Try changing the strings and retuning the ukulele to see if this fixes the problem.

USEFUL ACCESSORIES

Slip-resistant Cloth

"Cloth" is a 2mm thick layer of foamed material that is flexible enough to lie over your legs and also slip-resistant so that the ukulele won't move around too much. If you play sitting down, this is a great tool to stop the instrument moving sideways or turning. Of course, you'll still have to hold the neck a little bit, but coordinating your fretting and your picking hands while holding the ukulele should be easier with the cloth.

Thin cloths are usually deep black and look very elegant, but they are quite expensive and not so easy to come by. You can find good alternatives in crafts shops (sponge rubber is available in different colors) or hardware stores (slip-resistant mats for the trunk of a car).

Slip-resistant cloth and all alternatives can be cut into the required shape and size with scissors.

Cleaning materials from the household department of supermarkets are not recommended. Don't wash slip-resistant materials with cleaners that contain chemicals as they may damage the finish of your ukulele.

Classic slip-resistant cloth

Alternative: slip-resistant mat for trunk

Appendix

The Strap

You can buy special straps for the ukulele that are hooked onto the sound hole and go around your neck in a noose. This kind of strap holds the instrument when you're standing up, and you can easily remove one hand from the ukulele. Generally, while using this strap is beneficial, it is not as stable as a sitting position using a slip-resistant cloth. Also, the ukulele can fall forwards if you remove both hands. You also have to be careful with the hook on the sound hole as it can easily scratch the top of your instrument.

The strap by itself is a good solution if you have already found a good way to play standing without any other tools.

Ukulele Strap

The Guitar Strap

Just as with a guitar, a strap-pin can be placed on the bottom of the ukulele's rib. You'll probably see the spot where the two parts of the rib (the rolling sides of the ukulele) come together. Inside, there's a beam that the two wooden parts are glued to. This spot is quite strong and robust. If you'd like to screw in the pin yourself, make sure to pre-drill a small hole with a hand brace, although I'd recommend having a guitar maker or good guitar shop do it for you. The other end of the strap is attached to the head of the ukulele.

There are two strap-models by Caer that are similar to guitar straps and developed specially for the ukulele.

The biggest advantage of these kinds of straps is that the ukulele is safe around your neck and can't fall forward meaning that you can take both hands off the instrument and it will stay stable.

My Way of holding the Ukulele

Usually, I play sitting down using a combination of slip-resistant cloth and a footstool to find the best position. When I play standing up, I use a ukulele strap and a small piece of slip-resistant cloth which I put between the ukulele and my chest so the ukulele can't move sideways although the sitting position is always more stable.

Update since performing regularly:
I now play standing up most of the time and am using a strap attached to the endpin of my pickup on one end and the base of the neck.

"Footstool"

Tuner

I recommend that you get a tuner. The following features are important:

- Chromatic - it should be able to tune chromatically, so that you can use your ukulele in different tunings.
- Clip-On - I've had great experiences in noisy rooms with this kind of tuner. It's easy to attach, handy, and tunes very accurately despite other sounds and noises (although you may want to take it off before a concert for aesthetic reasons). Over the years branded tuners (i.e. by Korg) have worked well for me. Cheap tuners break easily and don't tune as accurately.
- Calibration - this is not absolutely necessary, but if you're playing with other instruments that are not so easy to tune (like a recorder in the hands of a beginner) it can be quite handy to be able to change the overall pitch of your tuner. Usually the tuner is set, so that A5 is tuned to 440 Hertz, but with a calibrated tuner you can change the note that is defined as A from around 320 Hz to 460 Hz.

Tuner

Appendix

DOWNLOAD

You'll find the audio tracks for this volume here:

www.poprockukulele.de/downloads

Fill in the form and click on the link! It'll take you to a dropbox folder. Find the link to the video playlist in the same folder.

If you have questions, ideas or problems, just write an email to:

info@poprockukulele.de

Made in the USA
Middletown, DE
20 October 2020